Stained Glass
Windows and Doors
Antique Gems for Today's Homes

Douglas Congdon-Martin

Schiffer Publishing Ltd

4880 Lower Valley Road, Atglen, PA 19310 USA

Library of Congress Cataloging-in-Publication
Data

Congdon-Martin, Douglas.
  Stained glass windows and doors : antique gems
for today's homes / Douglas Congdon-Martin.
      p. cm.
  Includes bibliographical references.
  ISBN 0-7643-2276-1 (hardcover)
1. Glass painting and staining—Collectors and
collecting. 2. Glass painting and staining in interior
decoration. 3. Glass painting and staining—United
States. 4. Glass painting and staining—England. I.
Title.

NK5304.C57 2005
747'.9—dc22
                                          2005023216

Designed by Mark David Bowyer
Type set in Zurich BT / Zurich BT

ISBN: 0-7643-2276-1
Printed in China
1 2 3 4

Published by Schiffer Publishing Ltd.
4880 Lower Valley Road
Atglen, PA 19310
Phone: (610) 593-1777; Fax: (610) 593-2002
E-mail: Info@schifferbooks.com

For the largest selection of fine reference books on
this and related subjects, please visit our web site at
www.schifferbooks.com
We are always looking for people to write books on
new and related subjects. If you have an idea for a
book please contact us at the above address.

This book may be purchased from the publisher.
Include $3.95 for shipping.
Please try your bookstore first.
You may write for a free catalog.

In Europe, Schiffer books are distributed by
Bushwood Books
6 Marksbury Ave.
Kew Gardens
Surrey TW9 4JF England
Phone: 44 (0) 20 8392-8585; Fax: 44 (0) 20 8392-9876
E-mail: info@bushwoodbooks.co.uk
Free postage in the U.K., Europe; air mail at cost.

Contents

Acknowledgments

This book was made possible by the generous contributions of several dealers in stained glass. They not only lent their collections, but were free with their time and expertise. Thanks go to:

Nick Chaffer owns "Step Back in Time" Antiques, in downtown Hightstown, New Jersey. Nick is a native of England and makes several trips a year to find antiques of interest to his American customers. His shop has a wide variety of quality items, but his specialty is definitely stained glass windows, and he always has a wide selection from which to choose. The shop is at 132 Franklin Street, Hightstown, New Jersey 08520 (1/2 mile west on Route 33 from Exit 8 of the NJ Turnpike. His phone is 609-426-1910 and his website is at www.englishhuntsmanantiques.com.

Joel Zettler owns Oley Valley Architectural Antiques in Adamstown, Pennsylvania. In business since 1973, Joel has seen hundreds of beautiful windows go through the shop, all of American manufacture. He always has a number on hand and offers the expertise a purchaser will welcome. His phone number is 717-335-3585 and his web address is www.oleyvalleyantiques.com.

Tom Crawford operates his business out of Allentown, Pennsylvania, and takes his windows to major shows around the northeast United States.

The Singletons opened their shop, The Stonehouse of Campbellville to me once again. Started in 1976, The Stonehouse is a treasure trove of stained glass, most of it from England. It is located at 8565 Guelph Line Road, Campbellville, Ontario. Their website is www.thestonehouse.ca. The phone number is 905-854-2152.

Joining the author in the photography for this book was Bruce Waters, assisted by Joe Riggio and Mark Bowyer.

Thanks also to the team at Schiffer Publishing for their continued support and talents.

Introduction

Stained glass was nearly a lost art by the early nineteenth century. From its high place in medieval cathedrals and manors, it fell into disuse and even outright disdain in the years that followed. Some segments of the Protestant reformation, including the Puritans in England, came to view statues and windows as idolatrous and in many instances destroyed the statues and smashed the windows, replacing them with clear, "white" glass. A cultural tragedy, indeed, stopped only because of the excessive costs involved in replacing the stained glass with clear glass.

In the case of the windows, it may also have been an educational tragedy. Besides their inherent beauty, stained glass windows were designed to tell the stories of the faith to what was, basically, an illiterate people. In their colorful "cartoons" the people could see the miracles being performed and learn the lessons of the parables. In more secular settings they could learn the ancient myths and legends as they were portrayed in glass. It is perhaps more than coincidence that the rise of printing technology and literacy corresponded with the decline of the art of stained glass.

Stained glass languished in the popular tastes and as an art for many years, until, by the eighteenth century, many of the ancient methods and formulae were lost. Fortunately there were some who continued to recognize and preserve the beauty of stained glass. Among them was Horace Walpole, who, by the 1740s, was collecting medieval glass from England and Europe. He hired one of the last craftsmen who knew the techniques of stained glass, William Price, to restore the glass and install it in his Rococo Gothic home at Strawberry Hill.

As England entered into the nineteenth century, its fascination with the romantic past increased and spawned the movement known as Gothic Revival. Swept up in this wave of interest was a renewed appreciation of stained glass. But with very little information passed down from the old artists, the nineteenth century glassmaker was at a loss. The unlikely rescuer of the art of stained glass was a lawyer named Charles Winston. A lover of stained glass, Winston wrote a book in which he reproduced the drawings of medieval stained glass. He also included in the book a description of the process of creating stained glass recorded by a German monk named Theophilus, in the first half of the twelfth century. The techniques Theophilus described were those used for medieval glass and, essentially, are those used today. They involved melting sand, potash, and lime together in a pot of clay and adding various metal oxides to create a colored glass that was, appropriately, called "pot metal" glass.

To find the "recipes" for the glass colors, in 1849 Winston sent shards of colored glass to a chemist for analysis, and forwarded the results to James Powell and Sons, Whitefriars Glassworks, where they were to produce excellent colored glass.

At the same time the architect Augustus Welby Northmore Pugin had become enamored of the Gothic ideal and developed a passion that was the driving force in the Gothic Revival of the early to mid-nineteenth century. Corresponding with the Oxford Movement in the church of England, which wanted to restore some of the ritual life of the church that it perceived as being lost, at its roots Gothic Revival was about restoring church architecture to the only "true" Christian architecture, medieval gothic, and a rejection of the neoclassical, pagan architecture then in vogue.

Stained glass, naturally, played a prominent role in Pugin's architecture, and he was a skilled designer of windows. Using traditional methods of painting the glass, and creating designs that were reminiscent of ancient designs, though not mere imitations, he used the windows as part of his overall Gothic design, both in churches and in secular buildings.

Pugin's ideas made their way across the Atlantic, and were adopted by American architects as well. By the late 1860s several major glass houses were producing stained glass for American churches and homes.

Domestic Stained Glass

The use of stained glass in domestic architecture was very limited until the mid-nineteenth century. It may have been found in some castles and in the homes of certain eccentrics (or visionaries) like Horace Walpole. The general unavailability of, and the lack of interest in, stained glass precluded its use in the everyday domicile.

The rediscovery of the glass formulas, the influence of Pugin and others, and the Industrial Revolution and the advances it brought to glass production, changed all this. In England and America, homes built in the Gothic Revival style were perfect platforms to accommodate stained glass.
According to H. Weber Wilson, the consequence of the rediscovery of colored glass, in America especially, was that it was "used here in more diverse and imaginative ways than ever before—the most creative result being the development and evolution of what is called American stained glass." (Wilson, page 1). The English may debate this conclusion, for there, too, the popularity of stained glass in domestic architecture grew throughout the last half of the nineteenth century and into the twentieth.

In both countries, colored glass was used to accentuate entryways and stairwells. Often the top portion of a doublehung window would be filled with a stained glass design, while the lower portion would be left clear, allowing a view of the surroundings. Above the front door one might find a eyebrow transom window with the house number worked into the design, and in larger entrances, a group of windows, transoms, and sidelights would frame the door with color and design. Stained or etched glass would also be used in water closets or other places where privacy was desired.

The Styles

Window design development follows the popular trends of architectural design as listed in the accompanying chart. Beginning with the Gothic Revival movement in the second quarter of the nineteenth century, nearly every design style incorporated stained glass.

It would be wrong, however, to conclude that a particular style window was limited to a particular style of architecture or a particular time period. Just as examples of architecture can be found well outside of their popularity, so windows of a variety of designs can be found in incongruous settings, depending on the taste of the architect or his client.

This book will attempt to place windows in their historical styles, tracing their development in both the United States and England. But the determination of where a particular window belongs is not an easy one and is subject to interpretation of various design elements. More than that, because of the slow diffusion of stylitic ideas from one place or time to another, some windows combine elements from various design motifs, confusing the issue even more. Furthermore, during transitional periods between one art movement and the next windows may exhibit characteristics of more than one style. During consultations leading up to the book's publication, various opinions were expressed that were at least as valid as the author's. Nevertheless, it may be helpful to see the common design elements and how various themes and motifs were used and varied from window to window.

Date	US	UK
1714-1830	Georgian Colonial	Georgian
1780-1840	American Federal	
1800-1830		Regency Style
1825-1890	Greek Revival/Classicism	
1825-1875	Gothic Revival/ Carpenter Gothic/ Wedding Cake (Faux Gothic)	Gothic Revival
1840s-1870s	Italianate	Italianate
1860-1870	Stick Style (Eastlake Style)	
1865-1885	Second Empire/Mansard	
1860-1890	Eclectic	Eclectic
1870-1880	Neo-Classicism	
1870-1910	Arts & Crafts	Arts & Crafts
1870-1910	Queen Anne (Shingle Style)	Queen Anne (Aesthetic)

A Word about Values

The values in this book represent what a consumer may expect to pay for a particular window when purchasing it from an antique dealer in the northeast United States. Prices vary from place to place, and from dealer to dealer, so this should be considered only a guide. As always, the best advice is to find an expert you trust and ask a lot of questions.

The value of stained glass windows is determined by several factors, some measurable and some related to aesthetics. Uniqueness, age, quality of the glass, and the presence of jewels and other special glass will, of course, enhance the window's value. The presence of two or more windows of the same design will generally bring a premium, since many homeowners like to use them as sets. On a more intuitive level the value can be affected by its overall beauty and intricacy, its palette or colorway, and the quality of the workmanship that went into it.

The bottom line then, is to look the window over carefully. Check for broken glass or caming that is in need of repair. And, perhaps most importantly, buy what you like.

This close up shows the rich colors developed by the 16th century glaziers. A field of painted quarry glass is accented with primary colors of red, green, yellow and blue.

16th century church window from England.

Details such as the saint's facial features were executed with a fine touch using monochromatic paints that were then fired for permanence.

A closer look at the details of the saint's figure.

Details such as the towers on either side of Gothic arch, are one of the reasons these Renaissance stained glass artists are so revered.

Gothic Revival
England & The United States

As discussed in the introduction, the Gothic Revival had its roots in England, and was championed, particularly by A.W.N. Pugin. In fact Pugin's father probably influenced his interest in the style. Fleeing from the French Revolution he settled in England and apprenticed in the office of the architect John Nash. At this time there was an interest in gentlemen's residences that were reminiscent of castles, i.e. in the Gothic style. Nash had no interest in Gothic design. Indeed he is quoted as saying "I hate this Gothic style; one window costs more trouble in designing than two houses ought to do." [Clark, page 123] The elder Pugin was assigned the task of creating these Gothic designs. His son followed him into design, but did not delve deeply into the Gothic style until 1834, when he became convinced that the Catholic Church was the true church and converted.

Along with his religious conversion Pugin also had a conversion in his design sensibilities. In his view the only true ecclesiastical architecture was in the Gothic style. He began designing buildings, furniture, and windows in this style, producing a stream of books in 1835 that would have a great impact on church architecture, and the architecture of public buildings (including the Parliament Buildings), and domestic structures.

Pugin designed many stained glass windows, usually in the medieval style, using quarry glass and painted details. Gothic Revival domestic architecture, naturally, was among the first to employ decorative stained glass.

Stenciled and hand-painted quarry glass church window typical of the Gothic Revival windows in England. From a church, the A in the lozenge at the bottom is for Alpha. There was a paired Omega window. 20.75" x 64". $2500-3000. *Courtesy of the Singletons, The Stonehouse of Campbellville*

Gothic Revival migrated to America quite quickly and found its way into church and public architecture. In the domestic area, it took more modest forms. The homes were generally of wood and featured steep roof pitches, ornate bric-a-brac trim, Gothic arches, and often porches. As in England, the first uses of stained glass in America were in these Gothic revival structures.

A close-up view of the cross motif.

Arch, with random pattern panes and painted shadowing. 23" x 21.25". England, $750-800. *Courtesy of the Singletons, The Stonehouse of Campbellville*

A painted violinist in the center of this colorful and unique window. United States, 23" diameter. It shows a close affinity with the artists of the 16th century, with its strong primary colors and painted details. $950-1050. *Courtesy of Joel Zettler, Oley Valley Architectural Antiques*

Two grape vine panels. While the foliage is painted in the traditional manner, the grapes are jewels, giving the window a particular brilliance. USA, mid-19th century. 12" x 25" and 11" x 26". $850-950 each. *Courtesy of Joel Zettler, Oley Valley Architectural Antiques*

Gothic arch window with painted baptismal font in round center. Pennsylvania, c. 1860. While the Gothic ideal may have been at work, the technique was lacking, both in design and in painting. 25" x 38". $650-750. *Courtesy of Joel Zettler, Oley Valley Architectural Antiques*

Painted Windows
in Victorian England and America

Moving away from the heavy painted windows of the Gothic Revival, what is generally known as the high Victorian period in both England and the United States, saw the evolution of Italianate, Mansard, and Eastlake styles. These were decidedly lighter in feel, and gave rise to new styles of stained glass windows.

Paint was still used, but now it was confined to medallions and other decorative elements within a window made up of an arrangement of geometric panes of quarry glass, sometimes highlighted by bull's-eyes or pressed jewels. The effect was uplifting and bright.

Two-panel Victorian window with painted lozenges at the center and painted quarries at the corners. As stained glass gained in popularity, windows such as this began to appear as decorative elements in domestic architecture. Generally less ornate, and certainly more secular than church windows, the techniques used to manufacture them were the same. Frames or borders of colored fillets were typical of the mid- to late 19th century windows both in England and the USA. England, 20.5" x 17" each panel. $1000-1200. *Courtesy of the Singletons, The Stonehouse of Campbellville*

"The Gatherer" is a wonderful painted window from England. The square medallion is surrounded by a field of quarry tiles, red fillets, and jewels. The outer border consists of tinted panes with etched star patterns in the red flash glass in the corners. 44.5" x 30.5". $1500-1750. *Courtesy of Nick Chaffer, Step Back in Time Antiques*

A close-up view of "The Gatherer."

Victorian pub windows. The red fillets define two areas in this window an the one that follows. In the upper portion here is a fillets circle containing a lozenge with a painted thistle. The lower portion in both windows has a pattern of diamonds and circles. England, 17" x 26.5". $750-850. *Courtesy of Nick Chaffer, Step Back in Time Antiques*

This small Pacis Nuncia painted window was probably from a church. Glass and paint are used to create an intricate frame around the central octagonal medallion. England, 18.75" x 13.25". $750-800. *Courtesy of the Singletons, The Stonehouse of Campbellville*

Pub window with a central lozenge of Acanthus leaves. England, 15" x 26". $600-700. *Courtesy of Nick Chaffer, Step Back in Time Antiques*

A close-up view of the dove.

Painted steamship in the medallion of a three-panel Victorian window. Each outer panel has a bull's-eye jewel at its center surrounded by painted flower panes and a frame of smaller pressed jewels. 29.5" x 14.25". England, $1200-1300 *Courtesy of Nick Chaffer, Step Back in Time Antiques*

A closer look at the boat painting.

A look at one of the flanking panels.

The round medallion of this rectilinear window is painted with daisies. 25.25" x 14". England, $500-600 *Courtesy of Nick Chaffer, Step Back in Time Antiques*

The bird is also the star of this window, but is surrounded by successive frames of painted glass. This may be an American window. C. 1880. 23" x 42.5". $850-1000. *Courtesy of Tom Crawford*

A favorite subject of Victorian windows were warblers and song-birds, such as the one decorating this medallion. England, 25.5" x 19". $900-1000. *Courtesy of the Singletons, The Stonehouse of Campbellville*

Scottish military Army Service Corps window with small jewels. This was one of several windows recognizing the various branches of the Scottish military units. The paint is exquisitely done and the border of fillets and dots is appropriate in its uniformity. Note shaped iron support. 21" x 21". $1450. *Courtesy of the Singletons, The Stonehouse of Campbellville*

Victorian window with etched flash glass and bull's-eye jewel center. Circa 1880. England, 20.25" x 19.75". 1 of 4. $650-750 each. *Courtesy of the Singletons, The Stonehouse of Campbellville*

A closer look at the etched and jeweled center.

The popularity of the song bird was also evident in American windows. Round window has also has a butterfly. U.S.A., 18" diameter. $950-1050. *Courtesy of Joel Zettler, Oley Valley Architectural Antiques*

A hand-painted Canadian window in the Gothic style depicting Easter lilies. 24" x 14". $650-750. *Courtesy of the Singletons, The Stonehouse of Campbellville*

Neo-Classicism

The Greek Revival period of American architecture evoked idealized images of that ancient and democratic civilization. Largely, however, it preceded the arrival of stained glass. In the years following the American Civil War, there was a revival of Neoclassicism. Classic pillars began to reappear on homes and gables once again reflected the lines of the Parthenon.

The windows of this period commonly featured a classical symbol, a wreath, torches, a fleur-de-lys, usually at the center of the window. The field was normally quite regular and geometric, creating an unobtrusive setting for the central symbol.

Similar designs occurred in English windows.

Flower wreath with a palmetto center. England, 30.5" x 18".
$500-600. *Courtesy of Nick Chaffer, Step Back in Time Antiques*

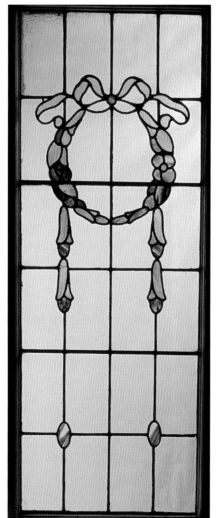

Flowery wreath. England, 19" x 51".
$450-550. *Courtesy of Nick Chaffer, Step Back in Time Antiques*

Left:
Arched window with Neoclassical wreath and Renaissance revival flourishes. England, 31" x 28.5".
$900-1000. *Courtesy of Tom Crawford*

Wreath around oval center. England, 22" x 26". $650-750. *Courtesy of Nick Chaffer, Step Back in Time Antiques*

Laurel wreath. England, circa 1900. 21" x 23". $500-600. *Courtesy of the Singletons, The Stonehouse of Campbellville*

Right:
Arched window with multicolored wreath and pendants. England, 32.75" x 58". $3000-4000. *Courtesy of the Singletons, The Stonehouse of Campbellville*

22

23

Half-rose pendants flanking a clear, white glass panel. England, 30" x 24,"
c. 1890. $550-650. *Courtesy of the Singletons, The Stonehouse of
Campbellville*

Left:
A swag and pendants. One of
a pair. English. $950 for the
pair. 17.5" x 42.75". $550-650.
*Courtesy of Nick Chaffer, Step
Back in Time Antiques*

Flowered ring with swag and pendants, with milkglass
jewels. Glasgow school with the subtle colors favored
by Mackintosh. 38" x 26". $1250-1350. *Courtesy of
Nick Chaffer, Step Back in Time Antiques*

A wreath and shield anchor the swag and pendants. England, 49" x
17". $550-650. *Courtesy of Nick Chaffer, Step Back in Time Antiques*

Shield in wreath with swags and pendants. Jewels are at the top of the pendants. England,
32. 5" x 18". $400-500. *Courtesy of the Singletons, The Stonehouse of Campbellville*

Central roses with a rose festoon and pendants. England, 50.75" x 29.25". *$1200-1300. Courtesy of Nick Chaffer, Step Back in Time Antiques*

Close-up of the double rose blossom.

Large arched window with double rose blossoms. England, 37" x 36". $2200-2500. *Courtesy of the Singletons, The Stonehouse of Campbellville*

This transitional window moves closer to the Neo-Classical mode, with its strong central figure and diminutive flourishes. USA, 35" x 13". $775-875. *Courtesy of Joel Zettler, Oley Valley Architectural Antiques*

A double palmetto in a multi-ringed circular form. USA, 24" x 24". $1475-1550. *Courtesy of Joel Zettler, Oley Valley Architectural Antiques*

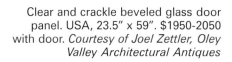

Clear and crackle beveled glass door panel. USA, 23.5" x 59". $1950-2050 with door. *Courtesy of Joel Zettler, Oley Valley Architectural Antiques*

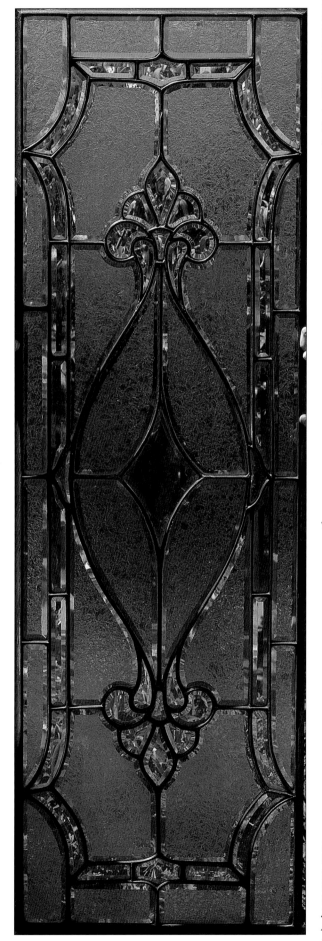

Textured glass transom address window. USA, 44" x 12". $475-525. *Courtesy of Joel Zettler, Oley Valley Architectural Antiques*

Clear, crackle, and textured glass sidelight with faceted jewels. USA, 12" x 44". $925-1000. *Courtesy of Joel Zettler, Oley Valley Architectural Antiques*

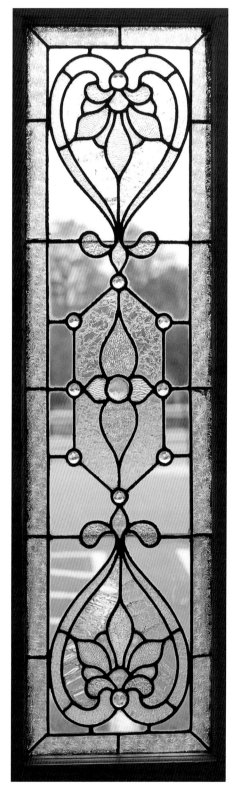

Clear and crackle beveled glass panel. USA, 20" x 62". $1475-1550. *Courtesy of Joel Zettler, Oley Valley Architectural Antiques*

Torch and wreath motif. Pennsylvania, 36" x 24". $775-825. *Courtesy of Joel Zettler, Oley Valley Architectural Antiques*

Right: Multicolored laurel wreath with ribbons and flourishes on clear textured glass field. USA, 72" x 30". $2950-3050. *Courtesy of Joel Zettler, Oley Valley Architectural Antiques*

Wreath and ribbons with crystal jewel at center. Pennsylvania, 28" x 36". $675-725. *Courtesy of Joel Zettler, Oley Valley Architectural Antiques*

Wreath and ribbon window. Pennsylvania, 40" x 27". $925-975.
Courtesy of Joel Zettler, Oley Valley Architectural Antiques

Laurel wreath and ribbons. USA, 36" x 14". $875-925.
Courtesy of Joel Zettler, Oley Valley Architectural Antiques

Wreath and shield. Pennsylvania, 40" x 30". $875-925.
Courtesy of Joel Zettler, Oley Valley Architectural Antiques

Wreath and ribbon monogram window. USA, 56" x 17.5". $575-625.
Courtesy of Joel Zettler, Oley Valley Architectural Antiques

Fleur-de-lys and swag with faceted jewel in the center. USA, 35" x 14". $675-725.
Courtesy of Joel Zettler, Oley Valley Architectural Antiques

Festoon and ribbons, with jewels. Pennsylvania, 55" x 48".
$1750-1850. *Courtesy of Joel Zettler, Oley Valley Architectural
Antiques*

Arched stained glass door with a multitude of design motifs, including a wreath, torches, ribbons, fleur-de-lys, and a banner. Pressed jewels are in the outer element. USA, 32" x 61". $4750-5000. *Courtesy of Joel Zettler, Oley Valley Architectural Antiques*

Swag with jewels. USA, 36" x 12". $875-925.
Courtesy of Joel Zettler, Oley Valley Architectural Antiques

A floral swag with ribbons on rectilinear field. USA, 44" x 15.5". $875-925. *Courtesy of Joel Zettler, Oley Valley Architectural Antiques*

Ribboned transom. Pennsylvania, 42" x 36". $775-825.
Courtesy of Joel Zettler, Oley Valley Architectural Antiques

Urn with flourishes. USA, 30" x 20". $775-825. *Courtesy of Joel Zettler, Oley Valley Architectural Antiques*

Urn with a burst of foliage on a rectilinear field. USA, 36" x 30". $925-1000. *Courtesy of Joel Zettler, Oley Valley Architectural Antiques*

Urn and swag motif. Pennsylvania, 41" x 24". $925-1000. *Courtesy of Joel Zettler, Oley Valley Architectural Antiques*

Vase and flourish motif. Pennsylvania, 36" x 18". $475-525.
Courtesy of Joel Zettler, Oley Valley Architectural Antiques

Clear textured glass and beveled glass with a shield and flourish pattern in the center. USA, 42" x 28". $1650-1750.
Courtesy of Joel Zettler, Oley Valley Architectural Antiques

Urn in an oval with fleur-de-lys flourishes. USA, 17.5" x 36". $775-825.
Courtesy of Joel Zettler, Oley Valley Architectural Antiques

While not an urn, this New York fruit basket with swags has the same Neoclassical feel. Zinc frame. 24.5" x 35". $925-1000. *Courtesy of Tom Crawford*

Detail

Shield and scroll. Pennsylvania, 58" x 19". $675-725. *Courtesy of Joel Zettler, Oley Valley Architectural Antiques*

Transom with shield. Pennsylvania, 40" x 17". $375-425. *Courtesy of Joel Zettler, Oley Valley Architectural Antiques*

Arched window with shell. USA, 24" x 26". $1150-1250. *Courtesy of Joel Zettler, Oley Valley Architectural Antiques*

Shield motif transom. Pennsylvania, 55" 19". $675-725.
Courtesy of Joel Zettler, Oley Valley Architectural Antiques

40

Crackle glass window with shield and flourish. USA, 27" x 32". $675-725. *Courtesy of Joel Zettler, Oley Valley Architectural Antiques*

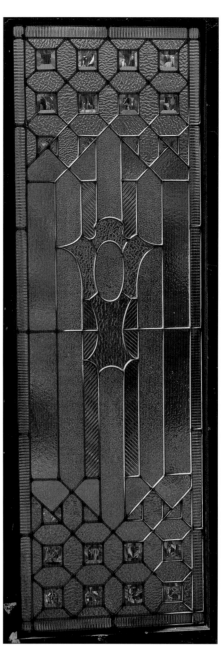

Textured and clear beveled glass window panel. USA, 20" x 60". $900-1000. *Courtesy of Joel Zettler, Oley Valley Architectural Antiques*

Shield and ribbon motif. Pennsylvania, 38" x 15". $475-525. *Courtesy of Joel Zettler, Oley Valley Architectural Antiques*

Shield motif with a multicolored flourish. Pennsylvania, 52" x 32". $1450-1550. *Courtesy of Joel Zettler, Oley Valley Architectural Antiques*

Fleur-de-lys motif. Pennsylvania, 21" x 25". $475-525. *Courtesy of Joel Zettler, Oley Valley Architectural Antiques*

Arched shield and palmetto design. USA, 20" x 29". $950-1050. *Courtesy of Joel Zettler, Oley Valley Architectural Antiques*

Oval window with fleur-de-lys. USA, 18" x 23". $825-900. *Courtesy of Joel Zettler, Oley Valley Architectural Antiques*

Wreath and fleur-de-lys window, American, c. 1890. Lancaster, Pennsylvania. 27.5" x 34.5". $1150-1250. *Courtesy of Joel Zettler, Oley Valley Architectural Antiques*

Fleur-de-lys and blossoms. USA, 48" x 25". $1150-1250. *Courtesy of Joel Zettler, Oley Valley Architectural Antiques*

Fleur-de-lys motif. Pennsylvania, 30" x 36". $475-525. *Courtesy of Joel Zettler, Oley Valley Architectural Antiques*

Textured and clear beveled glass door panel. USA, 25.5" x 60". $2750-2850 with door. *Courtesy of Joel Zettler, Oley Valley Architectural Antiques*

Torch design with ribbons. Pennsylvania, 17" x 38". $675-725. *Courtesy of Joel Zettler, Oley Valley Architectural Antiques*

Detail

Bowed window with crossed torches and roundel flames. USA, 24"
x 30". $875-925. *Courtesy of Joel Zettler, Oley Valley Architectural
Antiques*

Torch and ribbon motif. Pennsylvania, 55" x 19". $575-625.
Courtesy of Joel Zettler, Oley Valley Architectural Antiques

Four fleurs-de-lys in the center of this intricate duotone design. Pennsylvania, 43" x 30". $950-1050. *Courtesy of Joel Zettler, Oley Valley Architectural Antiques*

Eyebrow transom window in textured and beveled glass. USA, 58" x 14". $1250-1350. *Courtesy of Joel Zettler, Oley Valley Architectural Antiques*

Beveled clear glass arched transom window. USA, 48" x 14". $2850-2950. *Courtesy of Joel Zettler, Oley Valley Architectural Antiques*

Double-hung window with shield and wreath motifs in the top portion, and palmetto and flourishes in the bottom. USA, 32" x 60". $2550-2650 for the pair. *Courtesy of Joel Zettler, Oley Valley Architectural Antiques*

Clear beveled glass window. USA, 18" x 54". $1150-1250. *Courtesy of Joel Zettler, Oley Valley Architectural Antiques*

Beveled clear glass door panel with cut glass details. USA, 22" x 55". $1450-1550 with door. *Courtesy of Joel Zettler, Oley Valley Architectural Antiques*

Beveled etched and clear glass door panel, one of a pair. USA, 18.5" x 45". $1450-1550 with door. *Courtesy of Joel Zettler, Oley Valley Architectural Antiques*

Diamond patterned central panel in a door panel combining beveled white glass and various textures. USA. $850-950. *Courtesy of Joel Zettler, Oley Valley Architectural Antiques*

Beveled textured and clear glass door panel. USA, 20" x 60". $2750-2850 with door. *Courtesy of Joel Zettler, Oley Valley Architectural Antiques*

Textured and beveled glass door with a complex palmetto design in the center. USA. $1850-1950 with door. *Courtesy of Joel Zettler, Oley Valley Architectural Antiques*

49

Renaissance Revival

The flair of the Renaissance captured the imagination of the window designers of the late nineteenth century. They delved into flourishes and foliage with abandon, creating delightful windows in the process.

It is interesting that fewer English windows seem to have used this motif, and it may, perhaps, be attributed to the wider popularity of the Second Empire or Mansard styles on the western shores of the Atlantic.

Textured glass, jewels, and clear beveled glass make up this shield and flourishes arched window. USA, 71" x 16". $2950-3050. *Courtesy of Joel Zettler, Oley Valley Architectural Antiques*

White crackle and textured glass in a Renaissance Revival pattern. USA, 12" x 44". $950-1050. *Courtesy of Joel Zettler, Oley Valley Architectural Antiques*

Renaissance Revival sidelight. Pennsylvania, c. 1890. 15.5" x 61". $975-1025. *Courtesy of Joel Zettler, Oley Valley Architectural Antiques*

Heavily jeweled
Renaissance
Revival window.
England, 23.5" x
23.5". $975-1025.
*Courtesy of Tom
Crawford*

This semicircular Renaissance
Revival window has a
wonderful fleur-de-lys and
flourishes design. USA,
38" x 18". $2750-
2850. *Courtesy of
Joel Zettler, Oley
Valley Archi-
tectural
Antiques*

Large window showing the effective use of textured white glass accented by touched of color, in a dramatic came design. England, 57.5" x 53.5". $800-1000. *Courtesy of Tom Crawford*

An ornate, large, half-round window of cathedral glass. USA, 72" x 36". $9750-10,250. *Courtesy of Joel Zettler, Oley Valley Architectural Antiques*

Detail.

Foliate decorated window. USA, 14" x 48". $575-625. *Courtesy of Joel Zettler, Oley Valley Architectural Antiques*

Lyre and fleur-de-lys motifs fill this ornate window. USA, 29.5" x 32". $1450-1550. *Courtesy of Joel Zettler, Oley Valley Architectural Antiques*

An American window, probably from Lancaster, Pennsylvania, with the classical urn and Renaissance flourishes. 34.5" x 27.5". $1150-1250. *Courtesy of Joel Zettler, Oley Valley Architectural Antiques*

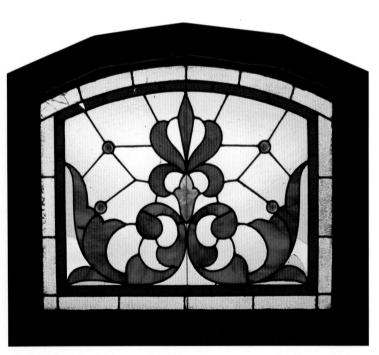

Arched window with stylized foliage. USA, 23" x 27". $775-825. *Courtesy of Joel Zettler, Oley Valley Architectural Antiques*

A fanciful foliage pattern peppered with jewels of many kinds and colors.
USA, 15" x 44". $1750-1850. *Courtesy of Joel Zettler, Oley Valley Architectural Antiques*

Top of a double hung window, showing fanciful flourish design typical of Renaissance Revival.
USA, 36" x 28". $725-775. *Courtesy of Joel Zettler, Oley Valley Architectural Antiques*

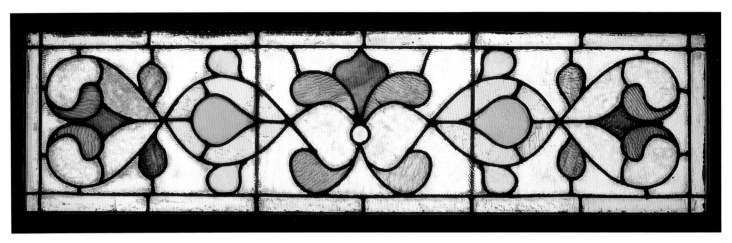

Wide transom. USA, 41" x 10.5". $925-975. *Courtesy of Joel Zettler, Oley Valley Architectural Antiques*

Double hung window. Pennsylvania, 27" x 60". $1350-1450 when repaired. *Courtesy of Joel Zettler, Oley Valley Architectural Antiques*

Scrolling pattern over two panels of random shapes with jewels, one of a pair. Pennsylvania. $1495 for the pair. *Courtesy of Joel Zettler, Oley Valley Architectural Antiques*

Pennsylvania window with oval center and foliate design. 30" x 18". $775-825. *Courtesy of Joel Zettler, Oley Valley Architectural Antiques*

Rectangular window with an abstract foliate design, also from Pennsylvania. 60" x 22". $1350-1450. *Courtesy of Joel Zettler, Oley Valley Architectural Antiques*

Oval window with segmented oval center, surrounded by a band of ribbon and jewels. USA, 24" x 39". $1950-2050. *Courtesy of Joel Zettler, Oley Valley Architectural Antiques*

The intricate oval uses waveform design and jewels. USA, 19.5" x 36". $2950-3050. *Courtesy of Joel Zettler, Oley Valley Architectural Antiques*

White beveled glass window with patterned glass and jewels. USA, 17.5" x 39". $2350-2450. *Courtesy of Joel Zettler, Oley Valley Architectural Antiques*

Geometric and Renaissance flairs, with jewels. Pennsylvania, 48"
x 17". $925-975. *Courtesy of Joel Zettler, Oley Valley Architectural
Antiques*

Lyre design, Pennsylva-
nia, 20" x 36". $525-
575. *Courtesy of Joel
Zettler, Oley Valley
Architectural Antiques*

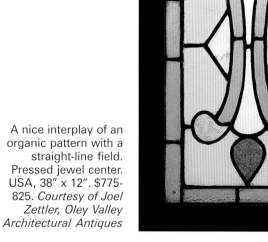

A nice interplay of an
organic pattern with a
straight-line field.
Pressed jewel center.
USA, 38" x 12". $775-
825. *Courtesy of Joel
Zettler, Oley Valley
Architectural Antiques*

Flowers and urn are surrounded by an oval in the center of this window. USA, 20" x 30". $1650-1750. *Courtesy of Joel Zettler, Oley Valley Architectural Antiques*

A star center in an oval, surrounded by fleur-de-lys patterns. USA, 19" x 30". $875-925. *Courtesy of Joel Zettler, Oley Valley Architectural Antiques*

Window with crest. USA, 24" x 37". $925-975. *Courtesy of Joel Zettler, Oley Valley Architectural Antiques*

Arched address transom. USA, 38" x 14". $675-725. *Courtesy of Joel Zettler, Oley Valley Architectural Antiques*

House number with scroll pattern. Pennsylvania, 31"" x 14". $375-425. *Courtesy of Joel Zettler, Oley Valley Architectural Antiques*

Number transom with scrolls. Pennsylvania, 34" x 15". $375-425.
Courtesy of Joel Zettler, Oley Valley Architectural Antiques

Pennsylvania window with inverted heart motif against Gothic arched panels. 26" x 18". $625-675. *Courtesy of Joel Zettler, Oley Valley Architectural Antiques*

House number transom with flourishes. Pennsylvania, 42" x 13". $375-425. *Courtesy of Joel Zettler, Oley Valley Architectural Antiques*

Diamond and jewels demi-round transom, with flourishes. USA, 32" x 17". $675-725. *Courtesy of Joel Zettler, Oley Valley Architectural Antiques*

Vase and foliage transom. USA, 40" x 16". $825-875. *Courtesy of Joel Zettler, Oley Valley Architectural Antiques*

Transitional Windows

As alluded to earlier, it is not always possible to limit a window to one time period or one design. A window may have the wreath of Neoclassicism coupled with the flourishes of the Renaissance Revival.

The results are interesting and delightful, and are appropriately found in the Eclectic architecture of both America and England.

Renaissance Revival motifs with the Greek palmetto of Neoclassicism and a fleur-de-lys, all blend together in this transitional window. USA, 16" x 38". $875-925. *Courtesy of Joel Zettler, Oley Valley Architectural Antiques*

Organic lyre and fleur-de-lys pattern with vines and blossoms. Pennsylvania, 48" x 18". $875-925. *Courtesy of Joel Zettler, Oley Valley Architectural Antiques*

Right:
Ornate cathedral glass window contains Renaissance and Classical elements. USA, 21" x 53". $950-1050. *Courtesy of Joel Zettler, Oley Valley Architectural Antiques*

American window in the Renaissance revival style, with palmetto and flourishes and an arch of jewels. Half of a doublehung window. 26.5" x 33.5". $895. *Courtesy of Tom Crawford*

Palmettos decorate the lyre in this transitional window. Pennsylvania, 26" x 29". $525-575. *Courtesy of Joel Zettler, Oley Valley Architectural Antiques*

Fleur-de-lys, ribbons, and a swag of faceted jewels make up this colorful, eclectic window. USA, 17' x 24". $775-825. *Courtesy of Joel Zettler, Oley Valley Architectural Antiques*

Strong Renaissance flourishes flank the central, palmetto in this wonderful transitional window with jewels. Pennsylvania, 53" x 26". $1850-1950. *Courtesy of Joel Zettler, Oley Valley Architectural Antiques*

A transitional window giving an Art Nouveau flair to
Renaissance elements. England, 34" x 17.75". $550-650.
Courtesy of Nick Chaffer, Step Back in Time Antiques

An Art Nouveau interpretation of the classic palmetto
motif. One of a pair of c. 1880 domestic windows. 24"
x 22". England, $2500-3000 for the pair. *Courtesy of
the Singletons, The Stonehouse of Campbellville*

Renaissance
flourishes in
a transitional
window.
One of pair.
England, 19"
x 47.25".
$1500 for
the pair.
*Courtesy of
Nick Chaffer,
Step Back in
Time
Antiques*

The classic palmetto design with an Art Nouveau interpretation decorates this double-hung window. England. Each frame, 31.5" x 31.25". $900-1100. *Courtesy of Nick Chaffer, Step Back in Time Antiques*

Edwardian heart design, c. 1890. England, 32.25" x 14". $450-550.
Courtesy of the Singletons, The Stonehouse of Campbellville

A three-panel English door with etched windows reflecting Classical and Renaissance motifs. Top panels, 11.5" x 11.5"; bottom panel 24" x 24".
Courtesy of Tom Crawford

Edwardian Windows
Prelude to Art Nouveau

The period generally known as the Edwardian Era, came at the end of Queen Victoria's long and fruitful reign and at a time of great creativity in design. William Morris's Arts & Crafts Movement had spawned some of the most creative designers of the nineteenth century and any other, and had effectively raised the art of domestic design to a high and respected level.

At the same time Rennie Mackintosh in Scotland was doing some groundbreaking work, producing time-less designs in a style reflective of Art Nouveau and looking forward to Art Deco.

The influence of Art Nouveau, born in France, was being felt throughout Europe, England, and even in the United States.

The windows of the Edwardian Era are generally lighter than their predecessors. They make use of white glass as a field for strong designs in brilliant colors. The subjects are generally geometric or abstract representations of blossoms and foliage. Many of the windows are influenced by Art Nouveau design, and some are wonderful representations of that form.

The Edwardian Era also saw the rise of the middle class in England, one of the fruits of the Industrial Revolution. All over the country housing was being built and much of it employed stained glass panels. It was not uncommon to see block after block of homes, each decorated with the same window designs. The quality of these windows was directly related to the quality of the home in which they were installed.

Palmetto design in the Art Nouveau mode. England, 43" x 24". $450-600. *Courtesy of Tom Crawford*

Organic flower forms and ribbons make up this colorful window. England, 33 x 21.5". $450-600. *Courtesy of Nick Chaffer, Step Back in Time Antiques*

The organic forms and sweeping lines in this Edwardian window give it a distinctly Art Nouveau air. England, $450-600. 33.5" x 22.25". *Courtesy of Nick Chaffer, Step Back in Time Antiques*

Stylized blossom. England, 37" x 17.25". $450-500. *Courtesy of Tom Crawford*

71

Freeform Edwardian window. England, 37" x 14". $450-550.
Courtesy of the Singletons, The Stonehouse of Campbellville

Edwardian window with textured glass throughout. England, 46" x 21".
$450-550. *Courtesy of the Singletons, The Stonehouse of Campbellville*

Heart and teardrop Edwardian window showing the Art Nouveau influence. England, 26.5" x 22". $450-550. *Courtesy of the Singletons, The Stonehouse of Campbellville*

Large rectangular
window with arched
design decorated with
abstract geometric
shapes in the
Edwardian mode.
England, 80" x 44".
$900-1100. *Courtesy
of Tom Crawford*

Rose and heart. England, 19.5″ x 13.5″.
$295-350. *Courtesy of Tom Crawford*

Heart and diamond motif with pendants. England, 40.5″ x 15.5″. $550-
650. *Courtesy of the Singletons, The Stonehouse of Campbellville*

Flower (tulip or trumpet) on a rectilinear field. England, 22.5" x 17.5".
$275-300. *Courtesy of the Singletons, The Stonehouse of Campbellville*

Tulip and hearts. England, 37" x 22.5". $550-650. *Courtesy
of the Singletons, The Stonehouse of Campbellville*

Edwardian window with trillium blossom and foliage. England, 24.5" x 22.5". $450-525. *Courtesy of the Singletons, The Stonehouse of Campbellville*

Left:
Edwardian side light with some hints of Mackintosh's design style. England, 17" x 53". $650-750. *Courtesy of Nick Chaffer, Step Back in Time Antiques*

Edwardian window with abstract blossom design. One of a pair. England, 24.5" x 20.76". $550-650 for the pair. *Courtesy of Nick Chaffer, Step Back in Time Antiques*

A window of the same basic design widened to double its width. England, 36.5" x 24". $650-750. *Courtesy of Nick Chaffer, Step Back in Time Antiques*

A heart and blossom window showing the Mackintosh influence. One of a pair. England, 18.25" x 24". $550-650 for the pair. *Courtesy of Nick Chaffer, Step Back in Time Antiques*

Art Nouveau influenced Edwardian window with a blossom.
One of a pair. England, 20.5" x 18.75". $700-800 for the pair.
Courtesy of Nick Chaffer, Step Back in Time Antiques

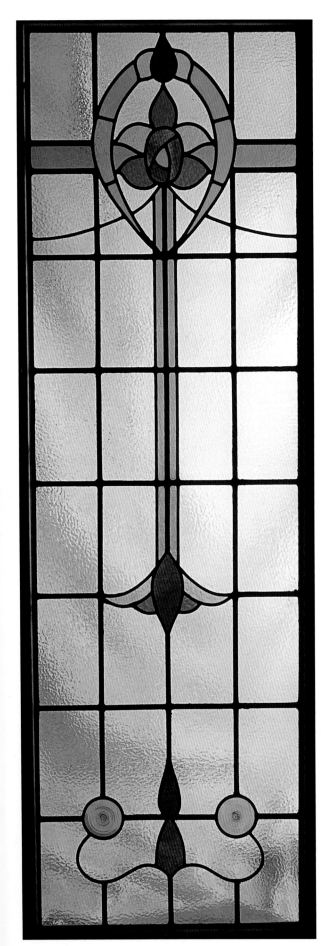

Large window with roses and jewels . England, 20.5" x 66.5". $550-600. *Courtesy of Tom Crawford*

Blossom in heart. England, 11" x 24". $225-275. *Courtesy of Tom Crawford*

Acorn. England, 32.5" x 34". $350-450. *Courtesy of Tom Crawford*

80

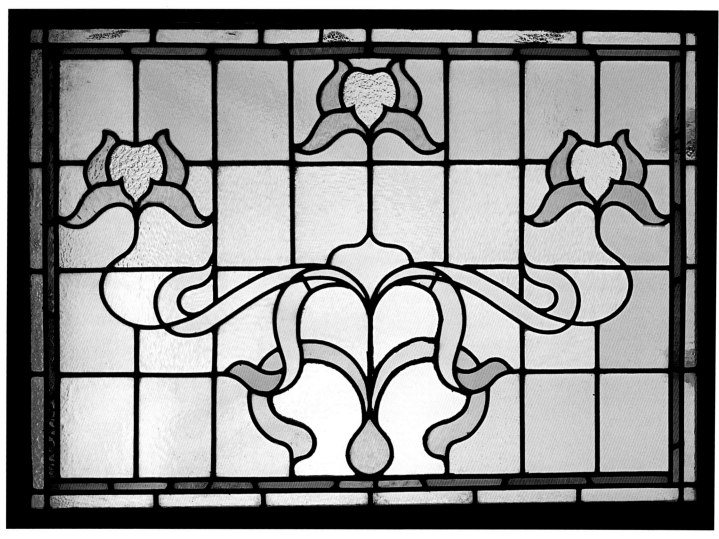

Lotus blossoms. England, 38" x 26". $900-1100. *Courtesy of the Singletons, The Stonehouse of Campbellville*

Heart and blossom. England, 15.25" x 22". $225-275. *Courtesy of Tom Crawford*

Detail.

Hearts. England, 22" x 36". $275-325. *Courtesy of Tom Crawford*

Detail of the floral work at the top.

Two-piece arched window. The lower portion has stylized blossoms and vines reminiscent of the Art Nouveau style, while the upper portion is a rather realistic portrayal of daffodils. England, 51.5" x 14". $900-1100. *Courtesy of the Singletons, The Stonehouse of Campbellville*

Detail of the Art Nouveau motif in the bottom panel.

Very rare red Art Nouveau iris with a bull's-eye jewel. One of a pair. England, 20" x 18.5". $750-950 for the pair. *Courtesy of Nick Chaffer, Step Back in Time Antiques*

Stylized blossoms grace the corners of this arched Art Nouveau design. England, 24.25" x 17.5". $300-375. *Courtesy of Tom Crawford*

Art nouveau lotus blossom, c. 1890. England, 26.25" x 18.5". $300-375. *Courtesy of the Singletons, The Stonehouse of Campbellville*

Art Nouveau window with red blossoms. England, 42.5" x 19.25". $700-800. *Courtesy of the Singletons, The Stonehouse of Campbellville*

Detail of the rose.

Art Nouveau blossoms. One of a pair. England, 17.5" x 19". $900 for the pair. *Courtesy of Nick Chaffer, Step Back in Time Antiques*

84

Tulip. England, 23" x 16". $325-395. *Courtesy of Nick Chaffer, Step Back in Time Antiques*

Art Nouveau blossom and foliage. England, 34" x 17". $325-395. *Courtesy of Tom Crawford*

Art Nouveau rose and blossoms. England, 18.5" x 15". $325-395. *Courtesy of the Singletons, The Stonehouse of Campbellville*

Art Nouveau floral design with vines and pendants, with heavily textured art glass. England, 36.5" x 16.5". $550-650. *Courtesy of Nick Chaffer, Step Back in Time Antiques*

Art Nouveau lily blossom. England, 18.25" x 20.75". $325-395.
Courtesy of the Singletons, The Stonehouse of Campbellville

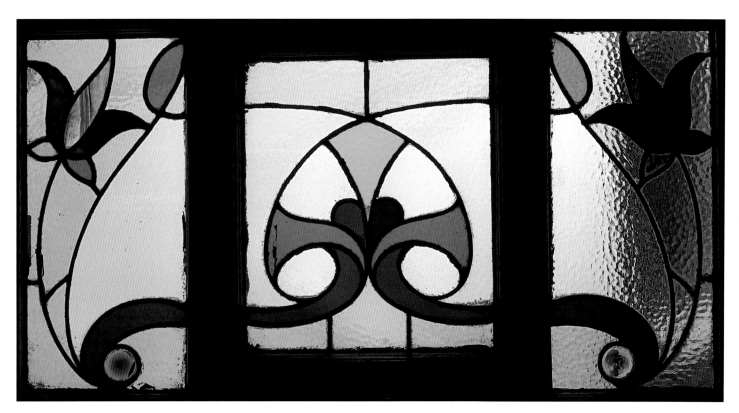

Three-panel Art Nouveau window with stylized palmetto in the center panel
flowers and bull's-eye jewels in the outside panels. England, 45" x 23". $550-
650. *Courtesy of the Singletons, The Stonehouse of Campbellville*

Right:
Art Nouveau window in
strong colors, c. 1880.
England, 32" x 22". $550-650.
Courtesy of the Singletons,
The Stonehouse of
Campbellville

Triangular rose. England, 13" x 13". $225-275.
Courtesy of the Singletons, The Stonehouse of
Campbellville

Close up of the
triangular rose.

Rose. England, 22" x 15.75". $275-325. *Courtesy of Nick Chaffer, Step Back in Time Antiques*

Art Nouveau window in organic form with interesting colorway and five jewels. England, 42" x 17". $750-850. *Courtesy of the Singletons, The Stonehouse of Campbellville*

Art nouveau window. The bottom half of a double-hung window, it has unusual shoulders at the top of the design, c. 1880. England, 29" x 21". $475-525. *Courtesy of the Singletons, The Stonehouse of Campbellville*

Tulip with jewels. One of as pair. England, 21.5" x 14.75". $900-1000 for the pair. *Courtesy of Nick Chaffer, Step Back in Time Antiques*

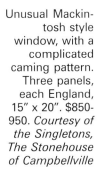

Unusual Mackintosh style window, with a complicated caming pattern. Three panels, each England, 15" x 20". $850-950. *Courtesy of the Singletons, The Stonehouse of Campbellville*

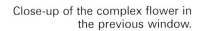

Close-up of the complex flower in the previous window.

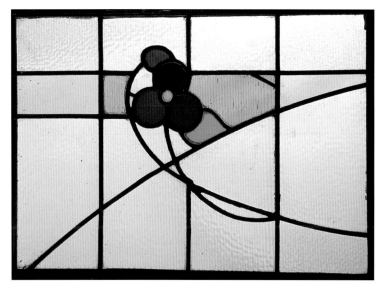

Clover, part of a multi-paneled window. England, 20.5" x 18.5". $225-275. *Courtesy of the Singletons, The Stonehouse of Campbellville*

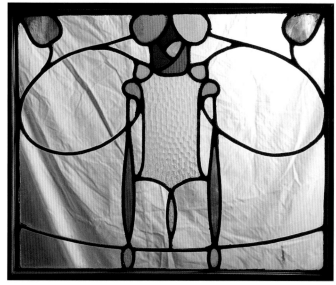

Rose and shield. England, 21" x 17". $425-500. *Courtesy of Tom Crawford*

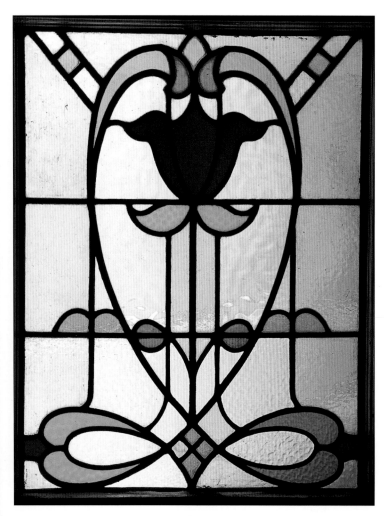

Tulip in a heart. England, 20.5" x 18.5". $395-475. *Courtesy of Tom Crawford*

A shield window in the Art Nouveau style exhibiting a nice use of bull's-eye jewels and patterned glass. England, c. 1900. England, 26" x 27". $500-600. *Courtesy of the Singletons, The Stonehouse of Campbellville*

Art Nouveau shield with thistles. England, 25" x 24". $500-600.
Courtesy of the Singletons, The Stonehouse of Campbellville

Art Nouveau three-part window. England. Central portion, 19.25" x 13", side pieces
19" x 13". $950-1050. *Courtesy of the Singletons, The Stonehouse of Campbellville*

Art nouveau, top of a double-hung. England, 49" x 23". $600-700.
Courtesy of the Singletons, The Stonehouse of Campbellville

Tulip in heart.
England, 50" x 17.5".
$275-325. *Courtesy of the Singletons, The Stonehouse of Campbellville*

The central piece of white glass in this Art Nouveau window is a large bull's-eye jewel. England, 20.75" x 16". $225-275. *Courtesy of the Singletons, The Stonehouse of Campbellville*

Double rose door panel. England,
21' x 41". *Courtesy of Tom Crawford*

A multicolored rose enlivens this window, along with the
swags and pendants. England, 26.75" x 21". $475-550.
*Courtesy of the Singletons, The Stonehouse of
Campbellville*

A close-up of a multicolored five-part
rose, with colorful foliage.

Round, four-part rose with contrasting center, and festoons with tear drop leaded pendants.
England, $425-475. *Courtesy of the Singletons, The Stonehouse of Campbellville*

Stylized rose and swag, with jewels. England, 29"
x 18". $225-295. *Courtesy of Tom Crawford*

Rose and swag. England, 22.25" x 12.75".
$225-295. *Courtesy of Tom Crawford*

Heart and swag. England, 17.5" x 11".
$175-225. *Courtesy of Tom Crawford*

Rose. England, 17" x 14". $200-255. *Courtesy of Nick Chaffer, Step Back in Time Antiques*

Arched window with central pattern, swags, and pendants. England, 39" x 22". $450-525. *Courtesy of the Singletons, The Stonehouse of Campbellville*

Three blossom window. England, 54.5" x 17.5". $375-425.
Courtesy of the Singletons, The Stonehouse of Campbellville

The central bunch of grapes is flanked by swags and bellflower pendants. England, 21"
x 12.25". $295-355. *Courtesy of Nick Chaffer, Step Back in Time Antiques*

Wreath and swag, one of a pair. England, 25.5" x 16". $550-650 for the pair. *Courtesy of Nick Chaffer, Step Back in Time Antiques*

Rose and swag. England, 33.5" x 16.5". $375-475. *Courtesy of Tom Crawford*

Rose and pendants. England, 22.75" x 21.25". $225-295. *Courtesy of Nick Chaffer, Step Back in Time Antiques*

Rose bud. England, 17.5" x 13". $155-200. *Courtesy of Tom Crawford*

Stylized rose with pendant, probably part of a multi-paned set. England, 11" x 20". $125-155. *Courtesy of Tom Crawford*

Blossom and pendant, with a jewel. England, 17" x 15". $255-325. *Courtesy of Nick Chaffer, Step Back in Time Antiques*

Three windows from a bow bay window, possibly from Yorkshire, UK. The central panel is a stylized shield with swags carrying the design to the outer panels with their lozenge centers. $1150-1350. *Courtesy of Nick Chaffer, Step Back in Time Antiques*

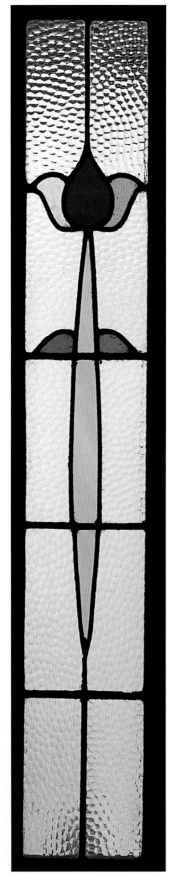

Rose. England, 15.25" x 13". $275-325. *Courtesy of Tom Crawford*

Stylized tulip side light. Circa 1920. One of pair. England, 6.5" x 42.75". $300-400 for the pair. *Courtesy of the Singletons, The Stonehouse of Campbellville*

A colorful interpretation of the fleur-de-lys. England, 16" x 16". $175-225. *Courtesy of Tom Crawford*

Window with six-part, square, stylized rose. England, 18.5" x 22.5". $225-265. *Courtesy of the Singletons, The Stonehouse of Campbellville*

Rose. England, 16" x 18.5". $225-265. *Courtesy of Nick Chaffer, Step Back in Time Antiques*

Close-up of the square, six part stylized rose. *Courtesy of the Singletons, The Stonehouse of Campbellville*

A close-up view of the round, four-part rose.

A four-part, round stylized rose with pendant and slight festoon. England, 18.75" x 23". $275-325. *Courtesy of the Singletons, The Stonehouse of Campbellville*

Rose. England, 27.25" x 14.25". $175-225. *Courtesy of Tom Crawford*

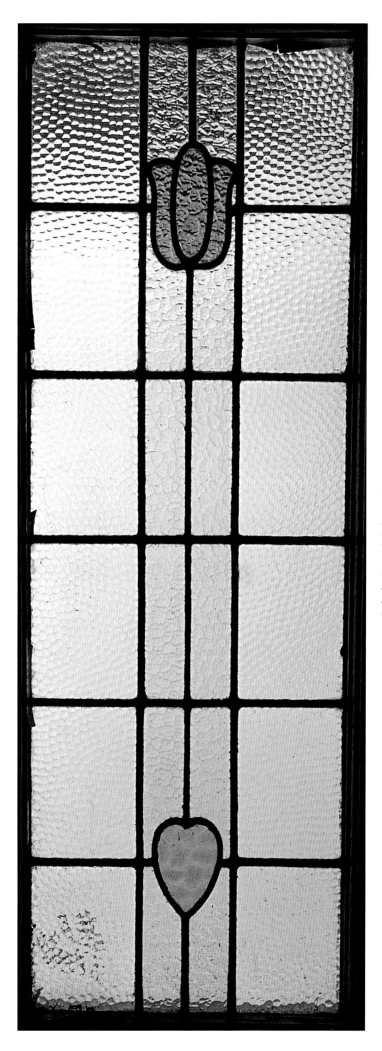

A tulip and a heart
grace this simple
window. England,
15" x 44". $275-350.
*Courtesy of the
Singletons, The
Stonehouse of
Campbellville*

107

Trillium in its simplest form. England, 18" x 10.75". $175-225.
Courtesy of the Singletons, The Stonehouse of Campbellville

Orange tulip in cathedral glass, deeply shaped white glass center. England, 18" x 17". $175-225. *Courtesy of the Singletons, The Stonehouse of Campbellville*

Red oval center and stylized leaves. England, 25.25" x 19". $175-225. *Courtesy of Tom Crawford*

Shield in oval. England, 20.5" x 31.5".
$225-275. *Courtesy of Tom Crawford*

Ivy and roses, with oval came,
c. 1940. England, 19" x 37.5".
$225-295. *Courtesy of Tom Crawford*

Geometric design. England, 21" x 37". $225-275. *Courtesy of Tom Crawford*

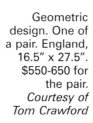

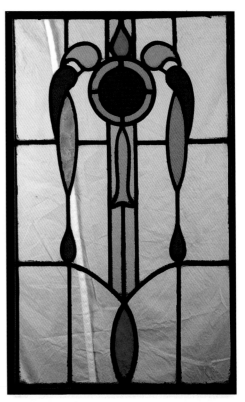

Geometric design. One of a pair. England, 16.5" x 27.5". $550-650 for the pair. *Courtesy of Tom Crawford*

Roses flank this shield with another below. England, 17.5" x 45". $475-575. *Courtesy of Nick Chaffer, Step Back in Time Antiques*

Abstract geometrical design. England, 28" x 17.25".
$195-250 *Courtesy of Tom Crawford*

Diamonds
and flares.
England,
37.5" x 16".
$325-425.
*Courtesy of
the Single-
tons, The
Stonehouse
of
Campbellville*

A circle and a segmented diamond
make up the medallion of this window.
England, 23" x 16". $175-225. *Cour-
tesy of the Singletons, The
Stonehouse of Campbellville*

An abstract pattern contrasts a square frame and flowing forms. England, 18" x 17". $125-150. *Courtesy of the Singletons, The Stonehouse of Campbellville*

Abstract design with red fillet border. England, 20" x 18". $225-295. *Courtesy of Tom Crawford*

Five-panel English door panel of tulips. Upper panels, 12" x 10"; lower panels, 7" x 26". *Courtesy of Tom Crawford*

Full length door panel with textured glass frame and abstract floral center. English, 21.5" x 66". *Courtesy of Tom Crawford*

Glass panel in a heavy English door. Cathedral glass and a bull's-eye jewel. 24" x 37". *Courtesy of Tom Crawford*

American Art Nouveau

The Art Nouveau movement also made its way to America and can be seen in the stained glass produced at the end of the nineteenth century.

Clear beveled glass door panel. USA, 24" x 55". $2650-2750 with door. *Courtesy of Joel Zettler, Oley Valley Architectural Antiques*

Trefoil and quatrefoil window.USA, 9" x 28". $475-525. *Courtesy of Joel Zettler, Oley Valley Architectural Antiques*

Rose vines with shield in circle. USA, 41" x 17". $1350-1450. *Courtesy of Joel Zettler, Oley Valley Architectural Antiques*

Sinuous tree with cathedral glass limbs and leaves and jeweled blossoms, one of a pair. USA, 24" x 24". $2950-3050 for the pair. *Courtesy of Joel Zettler, Oley Valley Architectural Antiques*

Arts & Crafts and Aesthetic Windows in England and America

In the late 1800s William Morris and Edward Burne-Jones gathered a group of like-minded people together. Their purpose was to bring true workmanship and design to a world that had given up those things to the world of mechanisation and mass-production. It was the birth of the Arts & Crafts Movement and a most creative era in English design.

The ideals of the movement quickly spread to America in the work of Elbert Hubbard and Gustav Stickley.

Stained glass was a vital part of Morris's work, and Burne-Jones created many wonderful windows in the Pre-Raphaelite fashion. Neither Stickley nor Hubbard produced windows, but they have a prominent place in the Craftsman homes that Stickley designed and promoted.

A closer look at the painted face.

This saint is typical of the painted work for churches in the late 19th century, and obviously influenced by the work of Byrne-Jones and other Pre-Raphaelites, though a much simpler design. It combines mosaic stained glass work with added details in paint, which are then fired on. English, 19" x 41.5". $1200-1500. *Courtesy of the Singletons, The Stonehouse of Campbellville*

Aesthetic Movement painted window in dome shape, probably a
fragment of a larger window. England, 22.75" x 12". $500-700.
Courtesy of the Singletons, The Stonehouse of Campbellville

The top portion of an Aesthetic Movement painted window, with arches, columns, and Tudor roses.
The glass work at the lower center whet ones curiosity for what the rest of the window may have
looked like. England, 36" x 14.5". $800-1000. *Courtesy of the Singletons, The Stonehouse of
Campbellville*

Left:
Two-panel painted window in the style of the Aesthetic
Movement. A combination of painted glass and mosaic work,
it uses the imagery of the Near East, a common theme of the
movement. Each panel 17" x 13.5". $1200-1500. *Courtesy of
the Singletons, The Stonehouse of Campbellville*

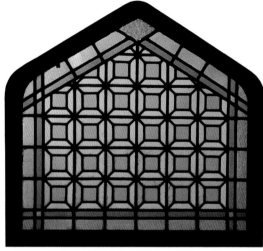

Arched window with quarry glass and star-textured glass at the apex. England, 24.5" x 22.5". $475-600. *Courtesy of the Singletons, The Stonehouse of Campbellville*

Gothic arch from a Manchester, England, church, c. 1890. 31" x 23". $450-550. *Courtesy of the Singletons, The Stonehouse of Campbellville*

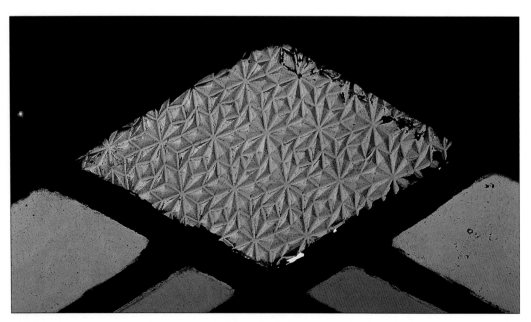

A close-up of the star-textured glass.

Two-part window with trefoil arch design. England. Top: 35.5″ x 31″; bottom: 35.5″ x 29.5″. $900-1100. *Courtesy of Tom Crawford*

Diamond with bull's-eye jewel center and smaller jewels at the corners. The white glass has a flowered texture. England, 16.5" x 16.5". $325-400. *Courtesy of the Singletons, The Stonehouse of Campbellville*

This diamond pattern has a blue bull's-eye jewel in the center and white jewels at the corners of the outer frame. England, 17.5" x 15.5". $475-575. *Courtesy of Nick Chaffer, Step Back in Time Antiques*

The blue lozenge center is surrounded by four bull's-eye jewels and filleted frames. England, 14" x 16". $450-550. *Courtesy of the Singletons, The Stonehouse of Campbellville*

Filleted lozenge with bull's-eye center. One of pair. England, 24" x 21.5". $500-600 each. *Courtesy of Nick Chaffer, Step Back in Time Antiques*

Two-panel window with bull's-eye jewel centers in the panels. England, 18"
x 19", each panel. $650-750. *Courtesy of Nick Chaffer, Step Back in Time
Antiques*

Heavy old window in a
typical geometric
design with five bull's-
eyes. c. 1870. One of a
pair. England, 15" x
22.25". $850-1000 for
the pair. *Courtesy of
Nick Chaffer, Step Back
in Time Antiques*

Geometric window with quatrefoil and jewel central blossom. England, 13" x 32". $375-475. *Courtesy of the Singletons, The Stonehouse of Campbellville*

Geometric design in round frame with white glass corners, probably custom made for a better home. The central lozenge is a bull's-eye jewel. This window is a wonderful example of the powerful use of caming as a design element. One of a pair, c. 1930. England, 20.5" x 20.5". $900-1100 for the pair. *Courtesy of Nick Chaffer, Step Back in Time Antiques*

A bull's-eye center jewel is surrounded by a quatrefoil and a filleted circle. Above and below the central medallion are textured jewels in a rose window pattern. England, 13" x 20.25". $400-450. *Courtesy of Nick Chaffer, Step Back in Time Antiques*

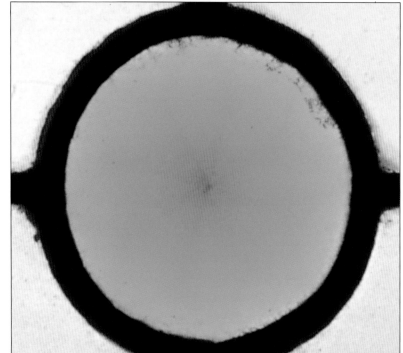

A closer look at the textured jewel.

Two-panel Victorian geometric window. Each panel has a bull's-eye center jewel. England, 27" x 15.5" each panel. $550-650. *Courtesy of Tom Crawford*

This simple, but beautiful cherry window gives hints of the Edwardian designs that were to appear in the very late 19th and early 20th centuries. One of a pair, 1900-1910. England, 16.5" x 15.25". $450-500 for the pair. *Courtesy of Nick Chaffer, Step Back in Time Antiques*

This Gothic arch, with flowers and jewels, is representative of the Aesthetic taste. England, 53.5" x 20". $3000. *Courtesy of the Singletons, The Stonehouse of Campbellville*

Made up largely of plain quarry glass, it has a red filleted frame and six white glass, bull's-eye jewels in the field. The flower medallion includes one pieced tulip blossom and one that is simply a jewel. England, 15" x 37". $650-750. *Courtesy of the Singletons, The Stonehouse of Campbellville*

Thistle medallion window with eight bull's-eye jewels. England, 40" x 20.5". $600-700. *Courtesy of the Singletons, The Stonehouse of Campbellville*

A close-up of the flower medallion.

Fleur-de-lys window with a filleted border and faceted round jewels in the field. England, 34.5" x 18". $450-550. *Courtesy of the Singletons, The Stonehouse of Campbellville*

This colorful arched window features a multicolored, bull's-eye center blossom and multicolored foliage. England, 23" x 20". $575-675. *Courtesy of the Singletons, The Stonehouse of Campbellville*

This variation on a Tudor rose has a faceted jewel center. England, 38" x 17". $375-475. *Courtesy of the Singletons, The Stonehouse of Campbellville*

Bud in geometric field. England, 21" x 19". $300-350. *Courtesy of Tom Crawford*

An interesting red and white medallion with blossoms, surrounded by colorful mixed patterns. England, 33.5" x 34". $1100-1300. *Courtesy of Nick Chaffer, Step Back in Time Antiques*

Pub window in geometric forms with two large bull's-eye jewels. England, 16" x 36". $375-475. *Courtesy of the Singletons, The Stonehouse of Campbellville*

Glasglow window with heavy bull's-eye jewels in the corners and jewels in the central design. The caming in this window shows the beginnings of the Art Nouveau influence. England, 32" x 32.5". $900-1100. *Courtesy of Nick Chaffer, Step Back in Time Antiques*

Medallion window with a bowing gentleman. England,
44" x 23". $550-650. *Courtesy of Tom Crawford*

Detail.

Transom showing elements of both Aesthetic and Edwardian
design. England, 51" x 14". $1200. *Courtesy of Tom Crawford*

"Owl" window with blue pressed jewel "eyes." England, 19.75" x 19.75". $450-550. *Courtesy of Tom Crawford*

A pub window in cathedral glass, c. 1950, shows how timeless stained glass and certain design trends can be. England, 9.75" x 32.5". $225-275. *Courtesy of the Singletons, The Stonehouse of Campbellville*

Coat-of-arms. England, 22" x 55". $375-450. *Courtesy of Tom Crawford*

Geometric with oval center and four jewels. England, 25.5" x 15". $625-700. *Courtesy of Tom Crawford*

Arched geometrical window from Pennsylvania. 12" x 30". $575-625. *Courtesy of Joel Zettler, Oley Valley Architectural Antiques*

Geometric Aesthetic design with pressed jewels. USA, 27" x 44". $950-1050. *Courtesy of Joel Zettler, Oley Valley Architectural Antiques*

Reflecting the Asian influence in the Aesthetic Movement, both in England and the USA is this bamboo trellis with foliage against a random pattern background. USA, 28" x 38". *Courtesy of Joel Zettler, Oley Valley Architectural Antiques*

A wreath gone wild! Two interlocking arches form a center circle around a pressed jewel. Pennsylvania, 51" x 23". $1450-1550. *Courtesy of Joel Zettler, Oley Valley Architectural Antiques*

The center of this window is a faceted blue jewel in a ring of conjoined fleur-de-lys. On either side is a vase with a plant. The filleted frames and bejeweled borders make this a typical American Aesthetic Movement window. 57" x 38". $5750-6250. *Courtesy of Joel Zettler, Oley Valley Architectural Antiques*

Sidelight with 18 bull's-eye jewels. USA, 10" x 36". $425-475. *Courtesy of Joel Zettler, Oley Valley Architectural Antiques*

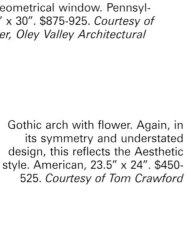

Arched geometrical window. Pennsylvania, 12" x 30". $875-925. *Courtesy of Joel Zettler, Oley Valley Architectural Antiques*

Gothic arch with flower. Again, in its symmetry and understated design, this reflects the Aesthetic style. American, 23.5" x 24". $450-525. *Courtesy of Tom Crawford*

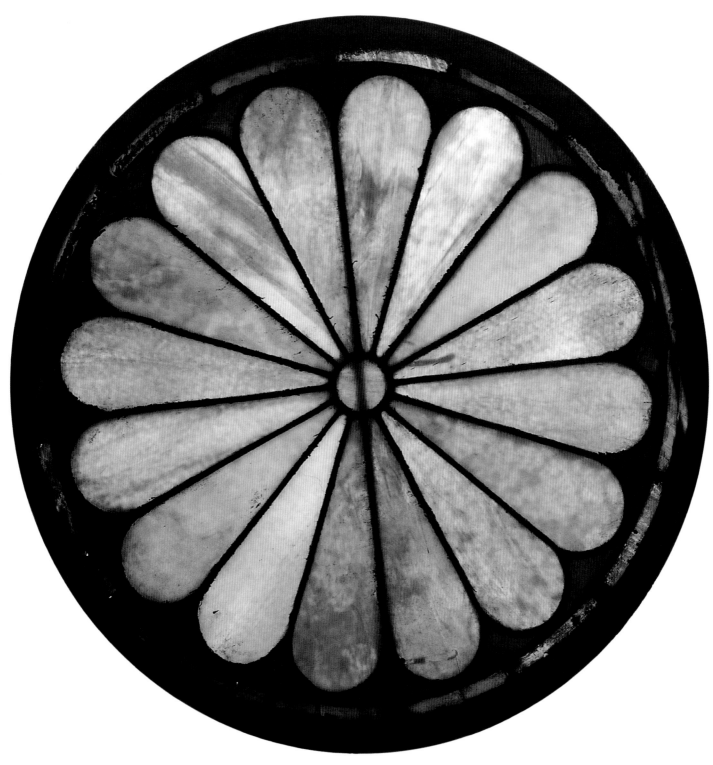

Rose window in cathedral glass. England, 23.5"
diameter. $675-725. *Courtesy of Tom Crawford*

A detailed look at the corner.

Aesthetic window with 9 jewels. Pennsylvania,
c. 1890. 24" x 33". $775-825. *Courtesy of Joel
Zettler, Oley Valley Architectural Antiques*

Transom with quatrefoil design. Pennsylvania, 38" x 16". $525-
575. *Courtesy of Joel Zettler, Oley Valley Architectural Antiques*

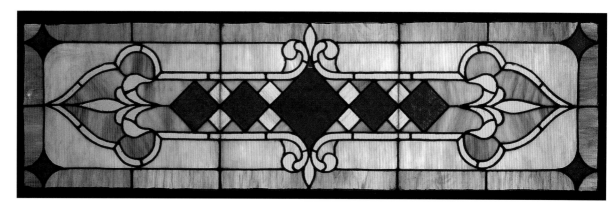

While Aesthetic in feel, this sidelight with diamonds and fleur-de-lys uses design elements from other styles. Pennsylvania, 20" x 60". $1450-1550. *Courtesy of Joel Zettler, Oley Valley Architectural Antiques*

Quatrefoil and fleur-de-lys with beveled diamond center door panel. USA, 24" x 40". $775-825. *Courtesy of Joel Zettler, Oley Valley Architectural Antiques*

Intersecting Gothic arches. USA, 32" x 13". $425-475.
Courtesy of Joel Zettler, Oley Valley Architectural Antiques

Arched door panel, using slag, tinted and textured glass. USA, 24" x 45". $2450-2350. *Courtesy of Joel Zettler, Oley Valley Architectural Antiques*

Diamond centered sidelight. USA, 20" x 60". $875-925. *Courtesy of Joel Zettler, Oley Valley Architectural Antiques*

Quatrefoil center. USA, 40" x 20". $725-775. *Courtesy of Joel Zettler, Oley Valley Architectural Antiques*

Semi-round transom window with star pattern. USA, 38" x 18". $675-725. *Courtesy of Joel Zettler, Oley Valley Architectural Antiques*

This eclectic semi-round transom exhibits strong colors and an interesting array of design elements including faceted jewels. USA, 32" x 16". $975-1025. *Courtesy of Joel Zettler, Oley Valley Architectural Antiques*

Eyebrow address transom. Pennsylvania, 30" x 16". $375-425. *Courtesy of Joel Zettler, Oley Valley Architectural Antiques*

Diamond and jewels center. 44" x 15.5". $975-1025. *Courtesy of Joel Zettler, Oley Valley Architectural Antiques*

A heart center with bull's-eye jewels and a white glass lozenge is flanked by shields. USA, 13" x 42". $575-625. *Courtesy of Joel Zettler, Oley Valley Architectural Antiques*

Diamond and jewels eyebrow transom with tulip and flourishes. USA, 32" x 14". $675-725. *Courtesy of Joel Zettler, Oley Valley Architectural Antiques*

Diamond and jewels center. USA, 27" x 15". $525-575.
Courtesy of Joel Zettler, Oley Valley Architectural Antiques

Arched transom with house numbers. Pennsylvania, 30" x 17". $275-325. *Courtesy of Joel Zettler, Oley Valley Architectural Antiques*

American window in cathedral and textured glass with four jewels.
USA, 23.25" x 17.5". $375-475. *Courtesy of Tom Crawford*

An oval segmented by diamonds in a yellow fillet frame and green cathedral glass border. USA, 30" x 16". $775-825. *Courtesy of Joel Zettler, Oley Valley Architectural Antiques*

An oval segmented by diamonds lies at the center of this square window. USA, 24" x 24". $775-825. *Courtesy of Joel Zettler, Oley Valley Architectural Antiques*

Arched geometric window. Pennsylvania, 36" x 27". $375-425. *Courtesy of Joel Zettler, Oley Valley Architectural Antiques*

White patterned glass panes are lined with cathedral glass triangles in this arched transom. USA, 22" x 12". $225-275. *Courtesy of Joel Zettler, Oley Valley Architectural Antiques*

Eyebrow clear glass pattern with spider web caming, framed by slag glass. USAS, 42.5" x 14.5". $275-325. *Courtesy of Joel Zettler, Oley Valley Architectural Antiques*

A pressed glass central lozenge is flanked by fleur-de-lys. USA, 34" x 14". $575-625. *Courtesy of Joel Zettler, Oley Valley Architectural Antiques*

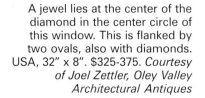
Two panels with diamond design and pressed jewels. USA, 32" x 47" overall. $875-925 each. *Courtesy of Joel Zettler, Oley Valley Architectural Antiques*

A jewel lies at the center of the diamond in the center circle of this window. This is flanked by two ovals, also with diamonds. USA, 32" x 8". $325-375. *Courtesy of Joel Zettler, Oley Valley Architectural Antiques*

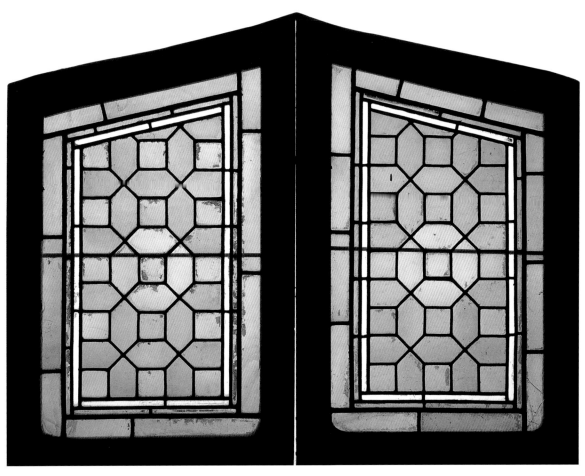

Two-piece cathedral glass window. Pennsylvania, 36" x 28" overall.
$775-825 for the pair. *Courtesy of Joel Zettler, Oley Valley Architectural
Antiques*

A repeating geometric pattern in cathedral glass with lozenge white glass
jewels, showing the slight color and design variations that occurred in
handmade glass. USA, 43.75" x 14.75". $475-525. *Courtesy of Tom Crawford*

Repeating abstract fruit pattern with variations. Pennsylvania, 28" x 12" ($675-725), and 43" x 12" (875-925). *Courtesy of Joel Zettler, Oley Valley Architectural Antiques*

A repeating geometric pattern in cathedral glass with lozenge white glass jewels. USA, 43.75" x 14.75". $475-525. *Courtesy of Tom Crawford*

Blossoms coming off of a heart and trefoil center design. Pennsylvania, 43" x 12". $525-575. *Courtesy of Joel Zettler, Oley Valley Architectural Antiques*

This eyebrow transom is graced with red tulips. USA, 30" x 8". 375-425. *Courtesy of Joel Zettler, Oley Valley Architectural Antiques*

Small Arts & Crafts rose window. USA, 13.2" x 13". $325-375. *Courtesy of Joel Zettler, Oley Valley Architectural Antiques*

Cluster of grapes with vine border. Pennsylvania, 24" x 32". $1175-1225. *Courtesy of Joel Zettler, Oley Valley Architectural Antiques*

A multicolored flower graces the center of this window. USA, 14" x 19". $525-575. *Courtesy of Joel Zettler, Oley Valley Architectural Antiques*

Two part arched window with a grapevine pattern in the lower portion. USA. Top: $775-825; bottom: $875-925. *Courtesy of Joel Zettler, Oley Valley Architectural Antiques*

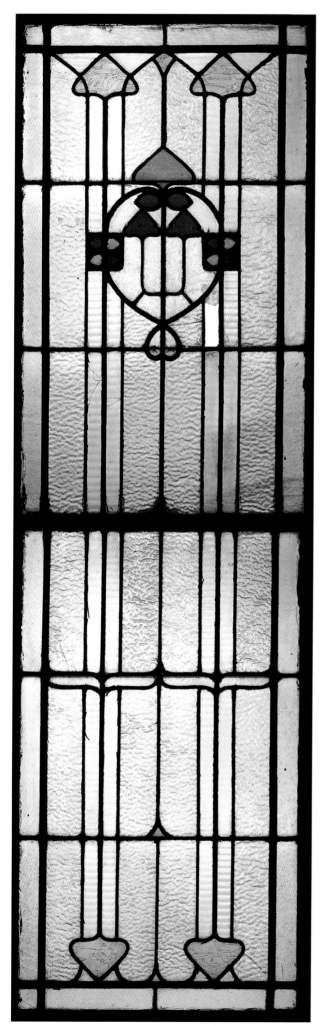

Detail.

Doublehung Mackintosh-
style window. Pennsylvania,
21" x 66". $875-925. *Courtesy
of Joel Zettler, Oley Valley
Architectural Antiques*

153

House number transom. Pennsylvania, 29" x 14". $275-325
Courtesy of Joel Zettler, Oley Valley Architectural Antiques

Eyebrow address window with flowers and
heart motif. Pennsylvania, 32" x 15". $375-425.
Courtesy of Joel Zettler, Oley Valley Architectural Antiques

Eyebrow transom, with diamond and jewel center with blossoms. USA, 41"
x 11". $575-625. *Courtesy of Joel Zettler, Oley Valley Architectural Antiques*

Arched transom with diamond and jewel center and flourishes. USA, 41" x 17". $875-925. *Courtesy of Joel Zettler, Oley Valley Architectural Antiques*

Semi-round transom with diamond and jewels center and flourishes. USA, 38" x 17". $775-825. *Courtesy of Joel Zettler, Oley Valley Architectural Antiques*

Blossoms and vines. USA, 58" x 12". $1175-1250. *Courtesy of Joel Zettler, Oley Valley Architectural Antiques*

A tulip in a circle graces the center of this window. USA, 44" x 15". $775-825. *Courtesy of Joel Zettler, Oley Valley Architectural Antiques*

Tulips and flourishes in this subtle earth-tone window. USA, 48" x 20". $1650-1750. *Courtesy of Joel Zettler, Oley Valley Architectural Antiques*

Shield in oval center. USA, 20.5" x 46". $975-1025. *Courtesy of Joel Zettler, Oley Valley Architectural Antiques*

Oval shield. Pennsylvania, 48" x 24". $775-825.
Courtesy of Joel Zettler, Oley Valley Architectural Antiques

Vine and blossoms. USA, 17.5" x 36". $725-775. *Courtesy of Joel Zettler, Oley Valley Architectural Antiques*

Eyebrow transom with intertwined vine and Arts & Crafts roses. USA, 11" x 41". $725-775. *Courtesy of Joel Zettler, Oley Valley Architectural Antiques*

Large eyebrow window with roses and vines. USA. $1350-1450.
Courtesy of Joel Zettler, Oley Valley Architectural Antiques

Stylized rose vine around a rectangular center. USA, 13" x 35. *$1450-1550.Courtesy of Joel Zettler, Oley Valley Architectural Antiques*

Repeating foliate pattern. USA, 26" x 16". $375-425. *Courtesy of Joel Zettler, Oley Valley Architectural Antiques*

Half of a double-hung window featuring a rose and foliage in a golden circle. USA, 26" x 26". $875-925. *Courtesy of Joel Zettler, Oley Valley Architectural Antiques*

Flowers and a heart decorate these transom windows. USA, 30" x 8" ($675-725) and 41" x 8" ($775-825). *Courtesy of Joel Zettler, Oley Valley Architectural Antiques*

A shield with a tulip graces the center of this airy design. USA, 27" x 37". $775-825. *Courtesy of Joel Zettler, Oley Valley Architectural Antiques*

Detail.

Art Deco

Officially the Art Deco movement was born in Paris in 1924, but it did not grow out of a vacuum. Rather it was a consequence of much prior work, including that of Rennie Mackintosh, Frank Lloyd Wright, and others.

Though most of the windows shown here predate the formal beginnings of Art Deco, they are clearly precursors of what would be a dominant style in the early twentieth century.

Art Deco rose with pendant. England, 26.75" x 36.5". $245-295. *Courtesy of the Singletons, The Stonehouse of Campbellville*

This window has a slightly arched top. The square blossom is a rather modernized element for a window made in c. 1890. The center of the blossom is cathedral glass. Faceted jewels decorate the pendants. England, 26" x 26.75". $295-355. *Courtesy of the Singletons, The Stonehouse of Campbellville*

Close-up of the Deco rose.

Art Deco shield. One of a pair. England, 19" x 26". $395-445 for the pair. *Courtesy of Nick Chaffer, Step Back in Time Antiques*

Deco arched window with sunburst pattern. England, 52" x 18.5". $325-395. *Courtesy of the Singletons, The Stonehouse of Campbellville*

Small deco window with chevron. England, 19.25" x 14.25". $125-175. *Courtesy of the Singletons, The Stonehouse of Campbellville*

Geometric Deco shield. One of a pair. England, 24.5" x 20.5". $295-350 for the pair. *Courtesy of Nick Chaffer, Step Back in Time Antiques*

Though this is English glass, it certainly resembles the American Prairie School style, with its rectilinear design and use of clear white glass. 19.75" x 39". $245-295. *Courtesy of the Singletons, The Stonehouse of Campbellville*

Deco window with chevron shield center. England, 36.5" x 17.5". $125-175. *Courtesy of the Singletons, The Stonehouse of Campbellville*

Deco design in bold colors. England, 18.25" x 11.25". $120-160. *Courtesy of the Singletons, The Stonehouse of Campbellville*

A stark Deco window with a chevron design. England, 18.5" x 28.5". $85-120. *Courtesy of the Singletons, The Stonehouse of Campbellville*

Geometric Deco window in pastel colors. England, 16" x 8.5". $85-120. *Courtesy of the Singletons, The Stonehouse of Campbellville*

Geometric design with jewels. England, 20" x 14". $125-175. *Courtesy of Tom Crawford*

The chevrons in this interesting window are of wide-fluted "refrigerator" glass. England, 15.25" x 34.5". $225-295. *Courtesy of the Singletons, The Stonehouse of Campbellville*

Wide-fluted glass. *Courtesy of the Singletons, The Stonehouse of Campbellville*

Two-piece window in the Deco style showing Egyptian motifs. England, 15" x 58.5" overall. $225-295. *Courtesy of the Singletons, The Stonehouse of Campbellville*

Art Deco cruciform window. One of a pair.
England, 18.5" x 15". $195-225 each *Courtesy of Nick Chaffer, Step Back in Time Antiques*

This Deco-like geometric window, c. 1910, is a bit ahead of its time, and retains some of the curves of the Edwardian period. England, 24.5" x 26.5". $475-525.
Courtesy of Nick Chaffer, Step Back in Time Antiques

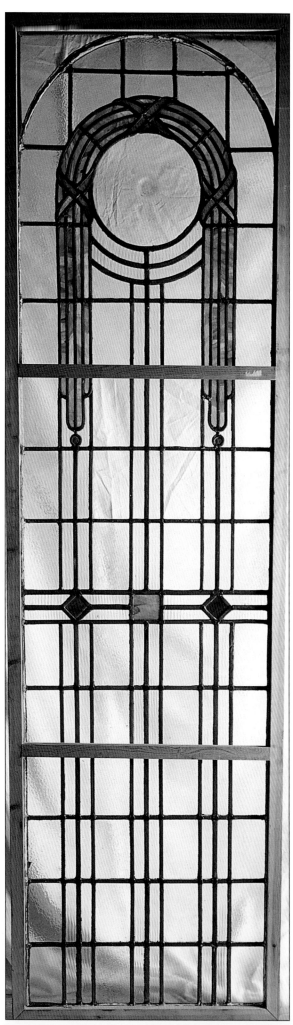

A stunning arched Deco window with an open wreath design echoes the classical motif. England, 24" x 89.75". $650-800. *Courtesy of Tom Crawford*

Figurative window in the Deco style, portraying a porpoise against setting sun. England, 24.75" x 44.5". $355-425. *Courtesy of Tom Crawford*

Oval center. England, 28" x 18". $250-300. *Courtesy of Nick Chaffer, Step Back in Time Antiques*

A Deco interpretation of the palmetto. England, 26 " x 19". $200-250. *Courtesy of the Singletons, The Stonehouse of Campbellville*

One of a pair of side windows. One of a pair. England, 14.75" x 46". $625-675 for the pair. *Courtesy of the Singletons, The Stonehouse of Campbellville*

Colorful Deco window. USA, 19" x 17". $475-525. *Courtesy of Joel Zettler, Oley Valley Architectural Antiques*

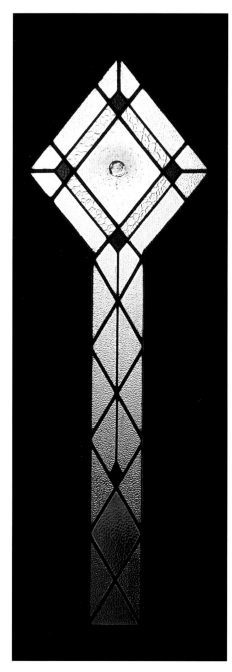

Art Deco door panel. The center of the top panel is a large bull's-eye jewel cut to shape. It is surrounded by a frame of textured white glass and red lozenges. English, 22″ x 66″. *Courtesy of Tom Crawford.*

Clear beveled glass door
panel. USA, 16" x 19".
$1750-1850 with door.
*Courtesy of Joel Zettler, Oley
Valley Architectural Antiques*

English Etched Windows

Not all decorative glass was colored. Talented etchers created scenic glass, such as that seen here, for use in homes and public buildings.

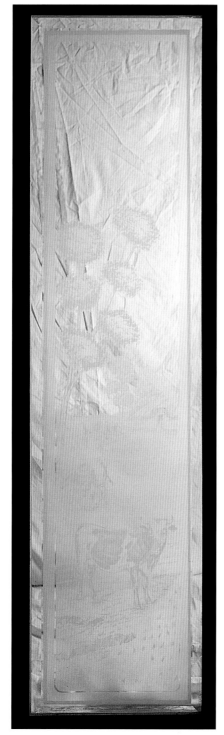

Etched window with cows and flowers, c. 1890-1900. England, 14.25" x 56.75". $750-1000. *Courtesy of Tom Crawford*

Etched window with swan. England, 17.5" x 53". $750-1000 *Courtesy of Tom Crawford*

American Figurative Glass

The popularity of Louis Comfort Tiffany gave rise to
many imitators, though few if any peers. The figurative style in American stained glass remains a
favorite to this day.

Three-panel landscape window with rising sun, tree and hills. Pennsylvania
68" x 36" overall. $4400-4600. *Courtesy of Joel Zettler, Oley Valley Architec-
tural Antiques*

Large landscape window. USA, 48" x 20". $4500-4600. *Courtesy of Joel Zettler, Oley Valley Architec-
tural Antiques*

A small landscape fills the shield of this window in the Classical form.
USA. *Courtesy of Joel Zettler, Oley Valley Architectural Antiques*

Detail.

A cathedral glass window with a shield and a scenic inset featuring a castle. USA, 24" x 48". $1450-1550. *Courtesy of Joel Zettler, Oley Valley Architectural Antiques*

Detail.

Sources

Aslin, Elizabeth. *The Aesthetic Movement: Prelude to Art Nouveau.* New York: Frederick A. Praeger, 1969.

Clark, Kenneth. *The Gothic Revival.* London: John Murray, 1995.

Congdon-Martin, Douglas. *Arts & Crafts Design for the Home.* Atglen, PA: Schiffer Publishing Ltd., 2001.

_____. *Arts & Crafts: The California Home.* Atglen, PA: Schiffer Publishing Ltd., 1998.

_____. *The Gustav Stickley Photo Archives.* Atglen, PA: Schiffer Publishing Ltd., 2002.

_____. *Old Stained Glass for the Home.* Atglen, PA: Schiffer Publishing Ltd., 2002.

Higgins, Molly. *Antique Stained Glass Windows for the House*, 2nd Edition. Atglen, PA: Schiffer Publishing Ltd., 2004.

Reyntiens, Patrick. *The Beauty of Stained Glass.* Boston: Little, Brown and Company, 1990.

Stained Glass Association of America. *SGAA Reference & Technical Manual.* Lee's Summit, MO: The Stained Glass Association of America, 1992.

Stickley, Gustav. *Craftsman Homes.* New York: Dover Publications, Inc., 1979.

Wilson, H. Weber. *Great Glass in American Architecture: Decorative Windows and Doors Before 1920.* New York: E.P. Dutton, 1986.

www.stainedglass.org. The website of the Stained Glass Association of America, and chock full of useful and interesting information.